DEATH

£2.00

by Karen Bryant-Mole

Consultant: John Hall,
Counselling Support Manager of ChildLine

Wayland

Designed by Helen White
Edited by Deb Elliott

We gratefully acknowledge the assistance of the following people
in the production of this book:
Dr Rachel Waugh, Principal Clinical Psychologist,
Great Ormond Street Hospital

All the words in **bold** are explained in the glossary on page 31.

This edition published in 1994 by Wayland (Publishers) Ltd

First published in 1992 by Wayland (Publishers) Limited
61 Western Road, Hove, East Sussex BN3 1JD

© Copyright Wayland (Publishers) Limited

British Library Cataloguing in Publication Data
Bryant – Mole, Karen
  Death. – (What's Happening? Series)
  I. Title II. Series
  306.9

HARDBACK ISBN 0-7502-0398-6

PAPERBACK ISBN 0-7502-1379-5

Phototypeset by White Design
Printed and bound in Italy by G. Canale & C. S. p. A.

CONTENTS

DEATH

Lisa was very upset when her dog, Bruno, died. She knew that all living things die in the end, but she had somehow hoped that Bruno would be different. Lisa knew that when something dies it can't come back again but her little brother, Sam, didn't understand. He kept saying '*Wake up Bruno, wake up*'.

Lisa cried and cried about Bruno. She couldn't stop thinking about him. She remembered when she had seen Bruno for the very first time. He was a tiny ball of fur with a little black nose. She remembered bringing him home and putting him in his basket. She remembered worrying about him the day he had been ill and taking him to the vet. She remembered all the times she had taken Bruno for a walk. He loved being outside. But now poor Bruno was dead.

Death is something that comes at the end of every life. We are all born, we live our lives and then we die. When people die they don't need their bodies any more and their bodies become like empty houses where the people used to live.

OPPOSITE Lisa had always known that Bruno would die one day. Death comes at the end of every life.

BELOW Bruno's death made Lisa feel very sad.

WHEN DO PEOPLE DIE?

BELOW *Shireen remembered her great-grandmother as being very old and tired (OPPOSITE).*

Shireen's great-grandmother died last year. She had been alive for a very long time. She was her mum's, mum's mum!

Whenever Shireen thinks of her great-grandmother, she remembers that she had to walk very slowly and she used to get tired quickly. Old people often die because their bodies have just become worn out. But it is not only old people who die. Sometimes much younger people die too. They may die because particular parts of their bodies have stopped working the way they should. It might not be something that can be seen. It could be something inside their bodies.

Sometimes people die because of an accident. They may have been in a car crash or knocked off a bicycle.

LEFT Shireen's great-grandmother died because her body had become worn out.

Although doctors can often make people well again, people sometimes die after accidents if their bodies get injured too badly.

I'M FRIGHTENED

BELOW After her mum died, Laura wanted to be with her dad all the time.

After her mum died Laura found it very difficult to go back to school. She made excuses about why she shouldn't go back, saying she had a headache or felt sick. She wouldn't let her dad out of her sight.

Laura was doing this because she was frightened.

She had loved her mum very much and her mum had died. Laura was frightened that her dad might die too.

When her dad realized what was worrying her they talked about what they could do. They decided to ask Laura's teacher if Laura could ring up her dad at playtimes, just to make sure that he was still all right. Laura's teacher understood how frightened she felt and agreed. At first Laura used to ring her dad every playtime. But after a while she didn't need to ring him quite so often and eventually she stopped feeling so scared all the time.

Sometimes children feel frightened for other reasons after someone they love has died. When his brother died James was scared that he was going to die too. He found night-times the most frightening. Many children feel lost and scared when someone they love dies.

If you feel confused or frightened try to talk to someone about it. If people know how you feel then they may be able to help you and talking about it might make you feel a bit better.

ABOVE Laura rang her dad every playtime to make sure he was all right.

9

IS IT MY FAULT?

Amy's grandfather used to live with Amy and her family. Everyone got on really well and Amy loved chatting to her grandfather about all the things she did at school. But sometimes she felt a bit cross about having to move into her sister's bedroom when he came to live with them and then she wished that he would just go away so that she could have her own bedroom back. When Amy's grandfather died all she could think about were the times that she had wished he wasn't there. Amy felt terrible. She felt that her wish had come true. It seemed to Amy as though it was her fault that her grandfather had died.

Like Amy, almost everyone has wished that someone would 'go away'. You might even have thought to yourself that you wished that someone was dead. But wishes and thoughts can't make someone die. It wasn't Amy's fault that her grandfather died.

Sometimes children think that the person they love died because they didn't love them enough or weren't good enough. Being naughty can't make someone die and being perfect can't stop someone dying.

Everyone says and does things that perhaps they wish they hadn't. It might also be helpful to try to think about the good times you had together and about the times you made each other happy.

OPPOSITE Amy loved her grandfather but sometimes she had wished he would go away.

I FEEL SO ANGRY

RIGHT Jonathan felt angry with the whole world when his mother died. It was all right for him to feel angry.

Many children feel very angry when someone they love dies. Sometimes children feel angry because there was nothing they could do to stop that person dying or angry that other people let it happen. They might even feel angry with the person who died.

Jonathan felt angry after his mum died but he kept it all to himself. He started getting stomach aches and then he began shutting himself away in his bedroom. His dad got very worried about him.

One day Jonathan dropped a model that he had made and it broke into two pieces. He started jumping on it and smashing it to peices. He was shouting and saying how much he hated the model. Then he said he hated his dad and his teachers and friends. Jonathan didn't really hate all those people though. He was just feeling very, very angry and saying he hated people was a way of showing that anger.

Jonathan's dad suggested taking a football down to the park. Jonathan kicked that football harder than he had ever kicked it before and every kick made him feel a little bit less angry. If you are feeling angry see if you can find a way to get rid of some of that anger. You could try thumping a pillow or bashing a ball with a bat. Do try to talk about the way you feel too.

BELOW If you feel hurt and angry, try thumping a pillow to let out some of your feelings.

I'M ALL MIXED UP

ABOVE Mark just wanted to feel safe and have someone look after him.

If someone you love dies you will probably feel very mixed up and upset.

Adults often want to help but sometimes, without really meaning to, they can muddle you up even more.

When Mark's dad died people told him that he was going to have to look after his mum and that he was the 'man' of the family now. But Mark was only nine and he didn't feel like being a man. If anything he felt like being a baby again. He wanted to feel safe and secure. He wanted someone to look after him. Adults sometimes don't know what to say when someone dies and perhaps they don't think hard enough about what they say and how it might make you feel.

After Ruth's grandmother died people said what a wonderful woman she had been and how cheerful and kind she was. Ruth missed her grandmother very much but she was confused. These people didn't seem to be talking about the same person she knew. Her grandmother often got angry and used to shout at children who played football in the street.

Often people only say good things about the person who has died because they are worried that people will think they are being rude.

If people say things to you that make you confused try to tell someone how it makes you feel and perhaps some of the muddle can be sorted out.

LEFT *After her grandmother died, people kept telling Ruth what a nice woman she had been. Ruth felt confused because, although she loved her grandmother, she knew she got pretty cross at times too.*

THE FUNERAL

After someone has died there is usually a **funeral ceremony**. Many funeral ceremonies are held in **religious** buildings such as **churches** or **mosques**. The body of the person who has died may be in a coffin. There might be music playing and someone usually speaks about the person who has died. You might see adults crying. That's because they are sad.

At the end of the ceremony the body of the person who has died is usually either buried or cremated. Being cremated means that the body is burned to ashes in a very hot fire. Being buried means that the body is put in a deep hole called a grave and covered with earth.

Luca had been very close to his grandfather and after his death Luca somehow thought that if he wished hard enough his grandfather might come back. He wouldn't listen when people tried to talk to him about his grandfather's death because he didn't want to believe it. Although it was a very sad moment, seeing the coffin made Luca realize that his grandfather really was dead.

Funeral ceremonies are a good way of showing everyone how much you love the person who has died. Often friends and relations come to the funeral ceremony to show how much they love and miss that person too. It is a chance to say goodbye to the person who has died.

OPPOSITE After the funeral, you can visit the person's grave. It might help you to feel close to them.

WHO'LL TAKE CARE OF ME?

Lots of children worry about what is going to happen to them when someone in their family dies.

Justine was very worried after her father died. What would they do without the money he had earned? She thought that they would have to sell the house and wondered where they would live. She didn't know how her mum would be able to afford to buy food for them. One evening she asked her mum whether ten year-olds could get jobs. When her mum asked why, Justine said it was the only way she could think of getting enough money to feed everyone.

Justine's mum hadn't realized that she had been worrying about things like this. She **reassured** Justine that everything was going to be all right. They didn't have a lot of money but they did have enough to live on and they wouldn't have to move.

Sometimes, though, someone's death may lead to a big change in the way you live. You might have to move house or move school. If you are feeling worried about things like this you will probably find it helpful to talk to someone about it. Although you might not like what you are told, most children find it better to know, rather than guess, about any changes that might happen.

OPPOSITE Justine talked to her mum about her feelings. Her mum reassured her that everything would be all right.

BELOW After her father died, Justine worried about how her family would manage.

19

WHAT HAPPENED?

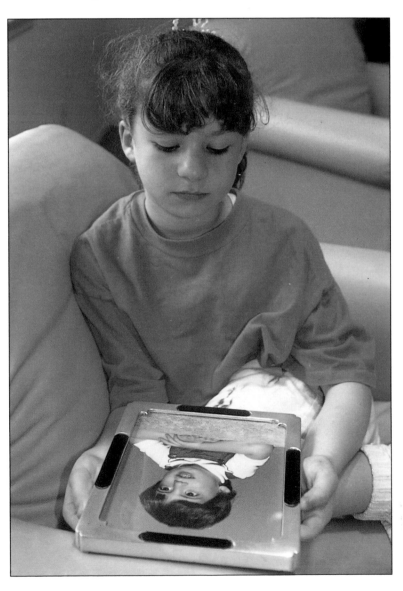

BELOW Sophie didn't know exactly how her brother had died, so she imagined all kinds of things.

After someone dies some children are frightened that they are going to die too. Knowing the reason that the person died might help to take away that fear.

Sophie's brother Tom died after being knocked over by a car. She kept asking her mum and dad questions about the accident but they were too upset to talk about it. All that Sophie remembered of that afternoon was waving goodbye to Tom and then being told by her mum a few hours later that he was dead. In between was a horrible gap. Because no one would tell Sophie what did happen, she was filling this gap with terrifying thoughts of what might have happened. Some days she thought of Tom lying in the road, his face covered with blood. Other days she thought of him screaming out in pain as he waited for an ambulance.

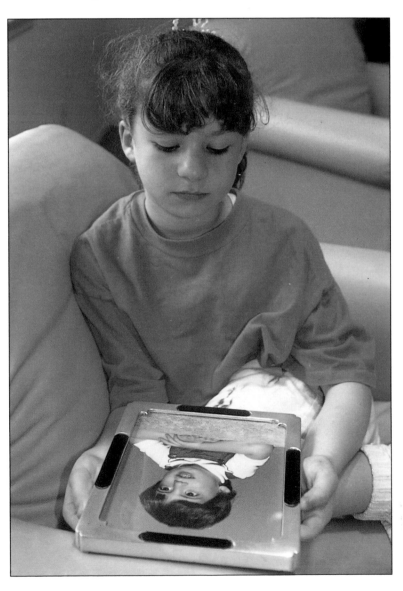

Eventually her mum and dad realized that not knowing the facts was making Tom's death even more upsetting for Sophie. They told Sophie that Tom hadn't died in pain. He had been knocked **unconscious** and so didn't feel anything. He was injured but there wasn't much blood. When Sophie heard this it felt as though the final piece of the puzzle had been put into place. Tom's life was now complete.

ABOVE Sophie talked to her mum and dad about Tom's death. Lots of children would like to talk about how and why the person they love died, but sometimes it is too painful at first.

21

TALKING ABOUT IT

ABOVE Greg felt very lonely after his mum died. Sharing his feelings with his dad made him feel less lonely.

When someone they love dies many children find that one of the most helpful things they can do is to talk about how they are feeling.

When Greg's mum died he found it hard to talk to his dad about how he felt. So, instead of talking, Greg started by just cuddling his dad. It made Greg feel very close to him. When Greg felt ready, he started trying to tell his dad about what was on his mind. Greg was worried that talking might upset his dad because he knew how much he was missing mum too. But his dad said it might make them both feel better to talk about how they were feeling.

One of the things he told his dad was that some-times he still talked to his mum, even though she was no longer alive. Greg was surprised when his dad said that he sometimes did too.

BELOW Greg and his dad looked at photographs of his mum and talked about the happy times they had together.

Many children long to talk about the person who has died. Sometimes adults think that talking about that person will only upset you and so they say nothing. But many children want to remind themselves of the person they love, even if it makes them feel very sad.

If you would like to talk about some-one who has died then just say so. Most people would be pleased to know that they can help you in this way.

DRAWING AND PLAYING

Sometimes it can be very difficult to put the way you are feeling into words.

Dean's sister Katie died after a long illness. He had known that Katie was going to die but when it happened he felt that somehow he wasn't ready. Dean had lots of different feelings and thoughts inside him that he couldn't really explain. His dad suggested that Dean might find drawing helpful.

At first Dean drew lots of dark pictures. There were often monsters in his pictures too. When he had finished these pictures he liked to scribble all over them and sometimes he even tore them into tiny pieces and threw them away. Dean was using these pictures to show how angry he felt about Katie's death and how cross he was that he hadn't been able to do anything to stop her dying.

ABOVE This is the sort of drawing Dean did at first.

You too might find it helpful to paint or draw. You might like to write about your feelings too. Or perhaps you might find it helpful to show people the way you feel by playing make-believe games. When someone they love dies, many children feel completely powerless.

They feel out of control and that can be worrying. If you paint or play you know that you can stop that picture or that game any time you want and you decide what happens next. You are in control of the game or the picture. That can feel very reassuring.

ABOVE Dean couldn't talk to anyone about his feelings, so he drew lots of pictures.

SPECIAL OCCASIONS

ABOVE Birthdays and the anniversary of the death can be difficult days for everyone.

After someone has died there will always be days when you particularly miss them. These might be days that are special to that person or days when you are celebrating something and think how good it would feel if that person was here too.

Helen's baby brother Josh was born with something wrong with his heart. He had lots of operations but, sadly, the doctors weren't able to save him and he died when he was six months old. Helen felt very upset. Josh had been so brave and even though he was only a baby he had been a real little person.

When it came to the time that would have been Josh's first birthday his mum and dad didn't know what to do. At first they thought that perhaps it would be best for everyone if they tried to forget the birthday. Then they realized that wouldn't be fair on anyone, especially not Josh. Trying to forget his birthday would be like trying to forget Josh and they didn't want to do that. So they decided to make it a very special family day. They looked at photos of Josh and they talked about his short life. They lit a candle for him and they cried because they missed him so much.

Even though it made Helen feel sad she was pleased that they had spent that day remembering Josh. It showed that, even though Josh was no longer with them, he was still important to them.

BELOW Helen's family decided to make Josh's birthday a special day.

THE FUTURE

When someone they love dies many children feel that they will never be happy again. It may seem to take forever but most children find that, in the end, they do start to feel better. The time after the death, before you start to feel better about it, is called **grieving**. For some people grieving takes a very long time.

Grieving and accepting the death of someone you love doesn't mean forgetting that person. Part of grieving can be finding good ways of remembering the person. You will probably have photos. You may have some special things that belonged to that person and most importantly of all you have your own **memories**.

If someone you love has died you may be feeling sad or angry or guilty or frightened. You may feel that your world has come to an end, but in time those feelings will probably pass. When that day comes, instead of feeling only sadness about the death of the person you love, you may be able to feel joy and happiness for the time you had together.

OPPOSITE *You don't have to forget the person. Keep some of his or her belongings to remind you of them.*

BELOW *It may take a while to accept that someone you love has died.*

FOR PARENTS AND TEACHERS

Following the death of someone they love, children, like adults, need to grieve. Sometimes adults think that the best way of helping a child to come to terms with the death is to avoid talking about it, in the belief that this will help the child 'get over it'. But death should not be thought of as something to 'get over'. It is better to think of grieving as a process to 'go through'.

If you are the parent of a child who has lost someone close to him or her, then it is likely that you are both experiencing similar feelings. Often, as adults, we try to suppress or even deny our emotions but in the long term this is not helpful. Allow yourself to feel frightened, cross or confused. Not only will this help you through the grieving process but it will help you to understand how your child is feeling too.

As a parent, teacher or friend, don't assume that because a child appears outwardly to be coping with the death that the same is true inwardly. We often find it difficult to talk about death, but for many people, both children and adults, talking is an important part of the grieving process. Let the child know that you are there when, and if, he or she wants to talk.

Organizations which support bereaved people include;
Cruse
Cruse House, 126 Sheen Road, Richmond, Surrey TW9 1UR
Tel: 081 940 4818

The Compassionate Friends
6, Denmark Street, Bristol BS1 5DQ
Tel: 0272 292778

Membership of The Compassionate Friends is open to all parents who have suffered the loss of a child, of any age and in any way.

GLOSSARY

Churches   Buildings where people who follow the Christian religion go to worship.
Funeral ceremony   When friends and family come together to say goodbye to the person who has died.
Grieving   Feeling very sad and unhappy because someone or something you love has died.
Memories   Things you remember from the past.
Mosques   Buildings where people who follow the Muslim religion go to worship.
Reassured   Comforted.
Religious   To believe in a god.
Unconscious   To be stunned or knocked out; usually as a result of an accident.

BOOKS TO READ

Death and Dying by Pete Sanders
(Gloucester Press, 1990)
Remembering Mum by Ginny Perkins and Leon Morris
(A&C Black, 1991)

INDEX

Picture Acknowledgements

The following pictures are from: Chris Fairclough 15; Jeff Greenberg 4, 5, 8, 9, 13, 17, 18, 19, 20, 21, 22, 23, 25, 28, 29; Zul Mukhida/Chapel Studios 7, 26, 27; Tony Stone Worldwide cover (Jo Browne/Mick Smee), 11 (Dan Bosler); Topham Picture Library 14; Wayland Picture Library 6, 12.

Some of the people who are featured in this book are models. We gratefully acknowledge the help and assistance of all those individuals who have been involved in this project.